Rookie
Read-About® Health

Chickenpox

By Sharon Gordon

Consultants
Nanci R. Vargus, Ed.D.
Primary Multiage Teacher
Decatur Township Schools, Indianapolis, Indiana

Jayne L. Waddell, R.N., M.A., L.P.C.
School Nurse, Health Educator, Lic. Professional Counselor

Children's Press®
A Division of Scholastic Inc.
New York Toronto London Auckland Sydney
Mexico City New Delhi Hong Kong
Danbury, Connecticut

Designer: Herman Adler Design
Photo Researcher: Caroline Anderson
The photo on the cover shows a child with chickenpox.

Library of Congress Cataloging-in-Publication Data

Gordon, Sharon.
    Chickenpox / by Sharon Gordon.
       p. cm. — (Rookie read-about health)
    Includes index.
    Summary: Provides a brief introduction to the effects of the chicken
pox virus, its possible prevention, and ways to make the patient more
comfortable.
    ISBN 0-516-22567-7 (lib. bdg.)   0-516-26871-6 (pbk.)
    1. Chickenpox—Juvenile literature. [1. Chicken pox. 2. Diseases.]
I. Title. II. Series.
RC125. G67   2001
616.9'14—dc21
                        2001002689

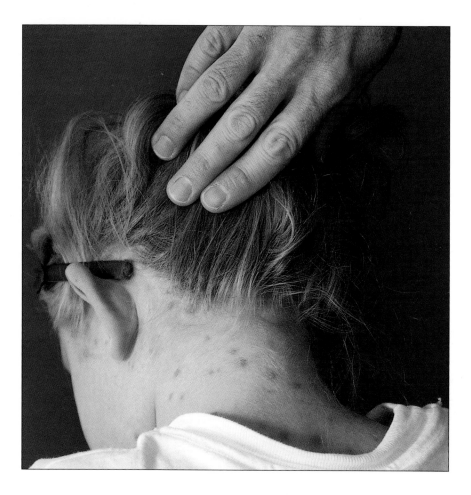

What is that red spot on
your neck?

You have the chickenpox!
Soon you will be covered
with spots.

Most people get chickenpox when they are children.

If you get it, your doctor will tell you to stay inside for about a week.

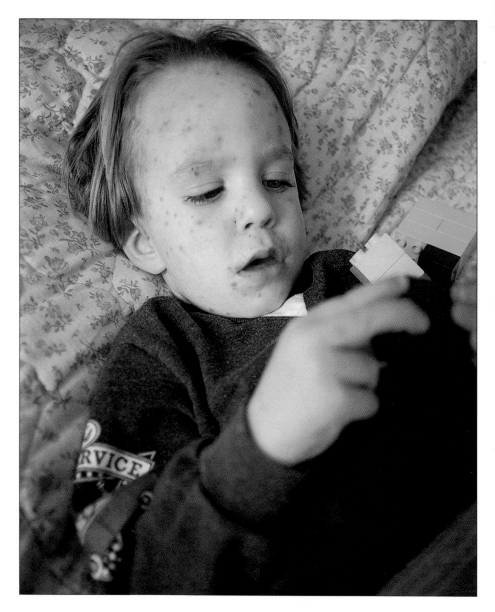

Chickenpox is a virus, or germ. It is easy to get and easy to give to others.

Today, many children get a shot that helps prevent chickenpox.

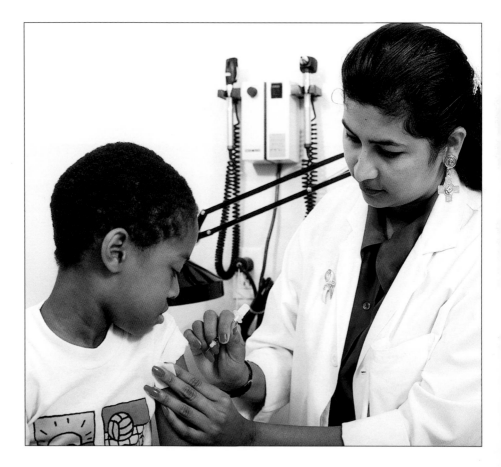

The chickenpox virus travels in the air. Other people can breathe it in and get sick, too.

That is why you cannot
go to school.

You may also have a cold or a fever when you get chickenpox. Your throat might be sore, too.

You might not feel like eating.

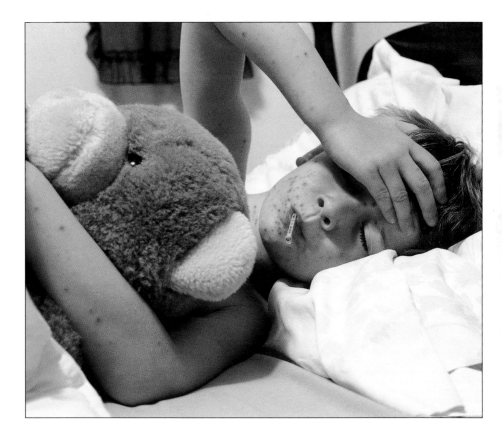

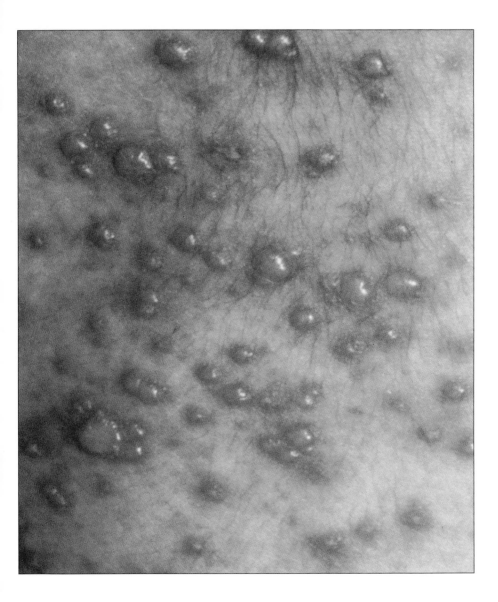

16

The spots will turn into blisters. They will begin to itch—really itch!

But do not scratch them!
You could get a scar.

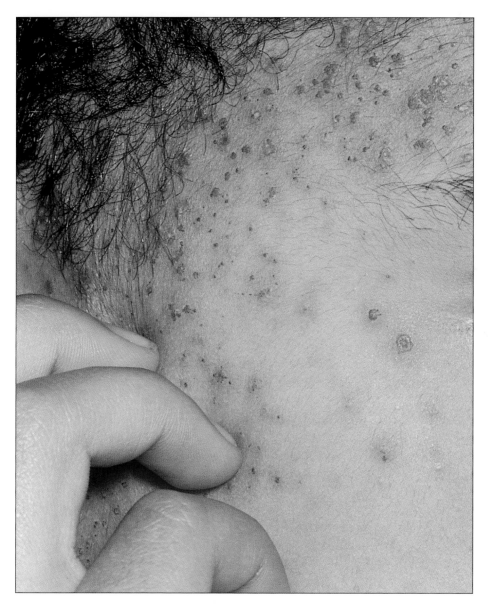

19

One way to stop the itch is to take a bath. It helps to add oatmeal or baking soda to your bath.

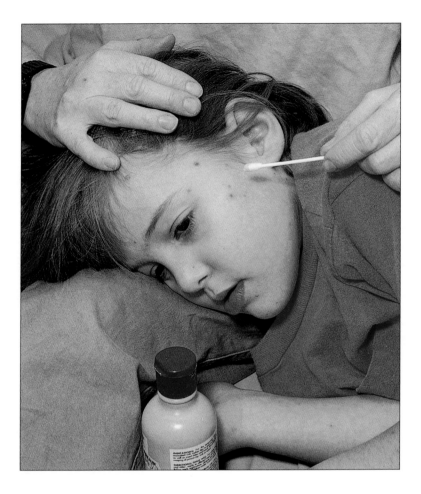

You can also put some
special lotion on the spots.

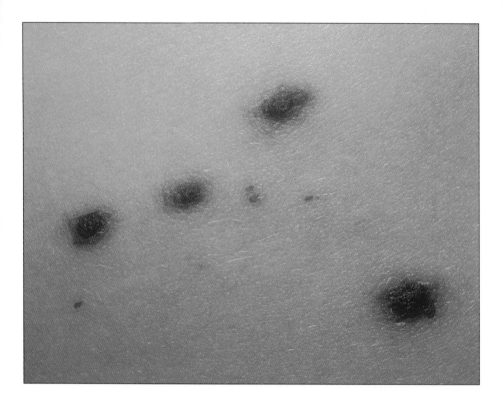

In a few days, you will
start to feel better. The
blisters will dry up and
become scabs.

Food will start to taste good again.

Now you can go back to school and see your friends!

The scabs will fall off
in about seven days.

You are all better now!
But do not put that lotion
away yet.

You never know who will be next!

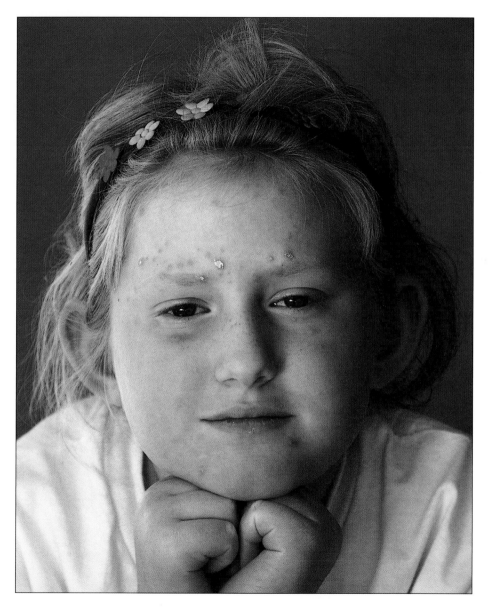

29

Words You Know

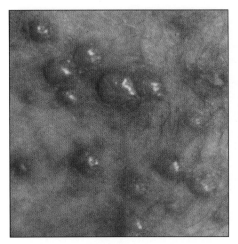

blisters

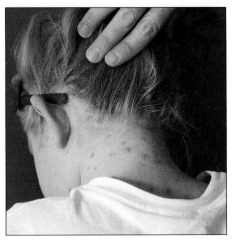

chickenpox

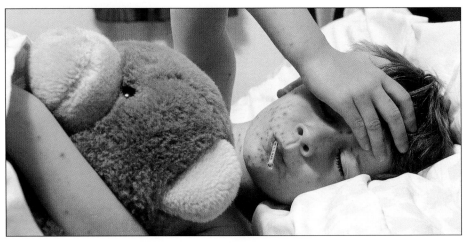

fever

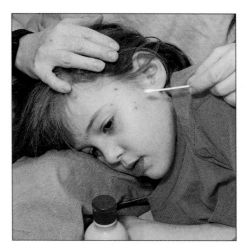

lotion

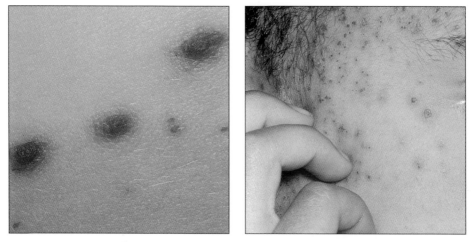

scabs

scratch

Index

About the Author

Sharon Gordon is a writer living in Midland Park, New Jersey. She and her husband have three school-aged children and a spoiled pooch. Together they enjoy visiting the Outer Banks of North Carolina as often as possible.

Photo Credits